THE OFFICIAL
Arsenal
ANNUAL 2017

A Grange Publication

Written by Josh James
Designed by B. Scott-Peterson

Manufactured and distributed under licence by Grange Communications Ltd., Edinburgh. Printed in the EU.

ISBN 978-1-911287-00-1

CONTENTS

Dear supporter,

Welcome to the Official Arsenal Annual 2017.

Last season was full of highs and lows. We eventually finished second in the table, to record our highest position for 10 years, but of course we all have regrets about how the season ended. We couldn't maintain our title challenge until the finish line, but I believe there was a lot to be proud of, and we want to build on those positives this year.

I was delighted to be able to sign Granit Xhaka, Lucas Perez and Shkodran Mustafi in the summer. These players have everything needed to be successful in the Premier League, and I believe they can all be major players for this club for many years to come.

We have also added some very promising young players, such as Rob Holding and Takuma Asano, who I expect to both develop rapidly over the next few seasons.

It means I have a very big and talented group to choose from. The key to success for us now will be togetherness. My players fight for each other, are full of ambition, and with our fans behind us too, I believe we can fulfill our potential and enjoy great success together.

In these pages you can read about our players for this season, look back on 2015/16 and test your knowledge in the quizzes and games.

We are all very proud of the values of Arsenal Football Club, and we know our fantastic supporters are a big part of what makes the club so great. So thanks for your fantastic support, enjoy the Annual, and keep cheering us on!

Arsène Wenger

ROLL OF HONOUR

League champions: 1931, 1933, 1934, 1935, 1938, 1948, 1953, 1971, 1989, 1991, 1998, 2002, 2004

FA Cup winners: 1930, 1936, 1950, 1971, 1979, 1993, 1998, 2002, 2003, 2005, 2014, 2015

League Cup winners: 1987, 1993

European Fairs Cup winners: 1970

European Cup Winners' Cup winners: 1994

Charity/Community Shield winners: 1930, 1931, 1933, 1934, 1938, 1948, 1953, 1991 (shared), 1998, 1999, 2002, 2004, 2014, 2015

2015-2016

AUGUST

THE SEASON STARTED WITH A BANG — and more silverware. Alex Oxlade-Chamberlain netted at Wembley Stadium as Arsenal retained the Community Shield with a 1-0 win over Jose Mourinho's Chelsea. When the real business began the following weekend though, the Gunners fell to earth with a bump, losing 2-0 at home to West Ham on the opening day of the Premier League season. The first win came away to Crystal Palace, with Olivier Giroud scoring an acrobatic opener. After a goalless draw at home to Liverpool, Arsenal completed the month with victory at St James' Park, thanks to a Fabricio Coloccini own goal – the second own goal in the team's favour in August.

RESULTS

Sun 2	Chelsea	N	1-0	Oxlade-Chamberlain	Community Shield
Sun 9	West Ham United	H	0-2		Premier League
Sun 16	Crystal Palace	A	2-1	Giroud, Delaney (og)	Premier League
Mon 24	Liverpool	H	0-0		Premier League
Sat 29	Newcastle United	A	1-0	Coloccini (og)	Premier League

ARSENAL.COM PLAYER OF THE MONTH:
FRANCIS COQUELIN

Season in Review

SEPTEMBER

ARSENAL CONTINUED TO CLIMB THE TABLE with a home win over Stoke City after the international break, but a controversial defeat at Stamford Bridge – in which Gabriel and Santi Cazorla were both sent off – checked their progress.

Mathieu Flamini was the unlikely match-winner as Arsenal started the Capital One Cup campaign with a memorable victory at the home of local rivals Tottenham.

Three days later there was a more familiar name on the scoresheet as Alexis Sanchez hit a hat-trick to inflict Leicester City's first defeat of the season. It would prove to be Leicester's only home reverse all year.

The Champions League campaign started in disastrous fashion though. Shock defeats away in Croatia and at home to Olympiacos meant Arsène Wenger's men were rock bottom of the group with no points from the opening two fixtures, and already faced an uphill struggle to qualify for the next round.

RESULTS

Sat 12	Stoke City	H	2-0	Walcott, Giroud	Premier League
Wed 16	Dinamo Zagreb	A	1-2	Walcott	Champions League
Sat 19	Chelsea	A	0-2		Premier League
Wed 23	Tottenham	A	2-1	Flamini 2	Capital One Cup
Sat 26	Leicester City	A	5-2	Walcott, Alexis 3, Giroud	Premier League
Tues 29	Olympiacos	H	2-3	Walcott, Alexis	Champions League

2015-2016

OCTOBER

AN EXPLOSIVE OPENING 19 MINUTES against Manchester United set the tone for an impressive October. Arsenal raced to a three-goal lead against United at Emirates Stadium, thanks to two goals from Alexis and one from Mesut Ozil. After the international break the Gunners recorded another 3-0 win – this time away to Watford – before attention switched back to the Champions League. The mighty Bayern Munich visited Emirates Stadium as the form side in Europe, having won all 12 games so far this season, scoring 39 goals in the process. But Arsenal recorded an unforgettable 2-0 win to keep alive their hopes of qualifying from the group stage.

A week later a much-changed side were knocked out of the Capital One Cup at Hillsborough, but the month ended with another 3-0 win – away to Swansea – to send Arsène Wenger's side to the top of the Premier League table. Joel Campbell scored his first Gunners goal in the game to cap an excellent run of form from the Costa Rican.

RESULTS

Sun 4	Manchester United	H	3-0	Alexis 2, Ozil	Premier League
Sat 17	Watford	A	3-0	Alexis, Giroud, Ramsey	Premier League
Tues 20	Bayern Munich	H	2-0	Giroud, Ozil	Champions League
Sat 24	Everton	H	2-1	Giroud, Koscielny	Premier League
Tues 27	Sheffield Wednesday	A	0-3		Capital One Cup
Sat 31	Swansea City	A	3-0	Giroud, Koscielny, Campbell	Premier League

STATS AND FACTS
Arsenal played 54 games in all competitions in 2015/16, winning 28

ARSENAL.COM PLAYER OF THE MONTH:
MESUT OZIL

Season in Review

NOVEMBER

BAYERN MUNICH GAINED REVENGE BACK IN GERMANY before Arsenal hosted the north London derby. Kieran Gibbs scored a priceless equaliser in the last 10 minutes to extend Arsenal's unbeaten run, and stay level on points with league leaders Manchester City. Defeat away to West Brom – in which Santi Cazorla missed a late penalty – was a setback, but Arsenal responded with a convincing home win over Dinamo Zagreb to stay on track in Europe. Mesut Ozil was in scintillating form, and he broke the deadlock in a man-of-the-match performance against the Croatians. Ozil scored again as a largely disappointing November concluded with a 1-1 draw at Norwich. As well as dropping two points at Carrow Road, both Alexis Sanchez and Santi Cazorla picked up injuries, and they joined Francis Coquelin in the treatment room for the next few months.

RESULTS

Wed 4	Bayern Munich	A	1-5	Giroud	Champions League
Sun 8	Tottenham Hotspur	H	1-1	Gibbs	Premier League
Sat 21	West Bromwich Albion	A	1-2	Giroud	Premier League
Tues 24	Dinamo Zagreb	H	3-0	Ozil, Alexis 2	Champions League
Sun 29	Norwich City	A	1-1	Ozil	Premier League

2015-2016

DECEMBER

ARSENAL RECORDED TWO OF THEIR BEST RESULTS of the season during December. After getting back to winning ways with a home victory over Sunderland in the Premier League, the Gunners travelled to Greece, needing to win by at least two goals to progress to the knock-out stages of the Champions League. A superb Olivier Giroud hat-trick – his first for the club – ensured Arsenal progressed to the business end of the competition for the 16th consecutive season.

Giroud scored again in a comfortable win at Villa Park, and the following week he was on the scoresheet again as Arsenal beat Manchester City in a crucial top-of-the-table clash, just before Christmas.

Boxing Day was not a day for celebration however, as Southampton ran riot with a 4-0 win at St Mary's, but the Gunners finished 2015 on top of the Premier League table, courtesy of a 2-0 home victory over Bournemouth. That win was memorable for Gabriel's first ever goal in Arsenal colours and for Petr Cech breaking the all-time Premier League clean sheet record with his 170th shutout.

RESULTS

Sat 5	Sunderland	H	3-1	Campbell, Giroud, Ramsey	Premier League
Wed 9	Olympiacos	A	3-0	Giroud 3	Champions League
Sun 13	Aston Villa	A	2-0	Giroud, Ramsey	Premier League
Mon 21	Manchester City	H	2-1	Walcott, Giroud	Premier League
Sat 26	Southampton	A	0-4		Premier League
Mon 28	Bournemouth	H	2-0	Gabriel, Ozil	Premier League

STATS AND FACTS
Seven players made their first-team debut during the season

ARSENAL.COM PLAYER OF THE MONTH: MESUT OZIL

10

Season in Review

> **ARSENAL.COM PLAYER OF THE MONTH: PETR CECH**

STATS AND FACTS
Olivier Giroud made the most appearances (53)

JANUARY

THE LEAD AT THE TOP-OF-THE-TABLE was extended to two points with a scrappy 1-0 win over Newcastle, but Arsenal were more convincing as they kicked off their bid for a third consecutive FA Cup. Sunderland took the lead at Emirates Stadium but Arsène Wenger's men hit back in style to extend the manager's 100 per cent record of making it past the third round.

It was Liverpool who came from behind in the next game, claiming a late equaliser in a thrilling 3-3 draw at Anfield, and there was another draw away to Stoke in the next match.

Per Mertesacker was sent off at home to Chelsea, as the Gunners fell to a 1-0 defeat, but goals from Calum Chambers and Alexis Sanchez were enough to see off Burnley at Emirates Stadium in the FA Cup fourth round at the end of the month.

RESULTS

Sat 2	Newcastle United	H	1-0	Koscielny	Premier League
Sat 9	Sunderland	H	3-1	Campbell, Ramsey, Giroud	FA Cup
Wed 13	Liverpool	A	3-3	Ramsey, Giroud 2	Premier League
Sun 17	Stoke City	A	0-0		Premier League
Sun 24	Chelsea	H	0-1		Premier League
Sat 30	Burnley	H	2-1	Chambers, Alexis	FA Cup

2015-2016

THE TITLE RACE BEGAN TO HEAT UP as we moved into February. Southampton keeper Fraser Forster was in amazing form to earn his side a goalless draw at Emirates, but the Gunners beat Bournemouth 2-0 on the south coast to set up a top-of-the-table clash with Leicester City. At half-time the Foxes led 1-0, which would have put them eight points clear of Arsenal with 12 matches remaining, but first Theo Walcott, then the returning Danny Welbeck – deep into injury-time – scored to grab a 2-1 win and reduce the deficit to two points.

The Gunners couldn't build on this momentum though. An uneventful goalless draw with Hull City in the FA Cup was followed by a 2-0 Champions League reverse at home to Barcelona, and worse was to come when Manchester United edged a five-goal thriller at Old Trafford.

RESULTS

Tues 2	Southampton	H	0-0		Premier League
Sun 7	Bournemouth	A	2-0	Ozil, Oxlade-Chamberlain	Premier League
Sun 14	Leicester City	H	2-1	Walcott, Welbeck	Premier League
Sat 20	Hull City	H	0-0		FA Cup
Tues 23	Barcelona	H	0-2		Champions League
Sun 28	Manchester United	A	2-3	Welbeck, Ozil	Premier League

STATS AND FACTS
Arsenal used 30 different players during the season, 16 of whom scored

ARSENAL.COM PLAYER OF THE MONTH:
MESUT OZIL

Season in Review

MARCH

ARSENAL'S TITLE HOPES SUFFERED A HUGE BLOW when Swansea came from behind to win 2-1 at Emirates Stadium, though three days later 10-man Arsenal scored a late equaliser through Alexis at White Hart Lane to halt the run of defeats, and dent Tottenham's own aspirations.

Two goals apiece from Olivier Giroud and Theo Walcott eased Arsenal past Hull and set up an FA Cup quarter-final clash at home to Watford. That's where Arsenal's defence of the trophy ended though, the Hornets claimed an unlikely 2-1 win on a hugely frustrating afternoon.

After Barcelona confirmed Arsenal's elimination from Europe, the Gunners bounced back with a solid 2-0 win at Everton. Academy product Alex Iwobi, making his first Premier League start just days after his full Champions League debut, was the star of the show, earning the man-of-the-match award and grabbing his first-ever senior goal.

RESULTS

Wed 2	Swansea City	H	1-2	Campbell	Premier League
Sat 5	Tottenham Hotspur	A	2-2	Ramsey, Alexis	Premier League
Tues 8	Hull City	A	4-0	Giroud 2, Walcott 2	FA Cup
Sun 13	Watford	H	1-2	Welbeck	FA Cup
Wed 16	Barcelona	A	1-3	Elneny	Champions League
Sat 19	Everton	A	2-0	Welbeck, Iwobi	Premier League

2015-2016

ALEX IWOBI WAS AMONG THE SCORERS AGAIN as April began with a thumping 4-0 win over Watford, but following back-to-back draws with West Ham and Crystal Palace, the extent of Arsenal's ambitions now looked to be a top-four finish, with Leicester 13 points ahead at the summit.

In-form Alexis scored his fifth goal in four games, proving he had put his injury problems well and truly behind him, with a brace in the home win over West Brom. After a goalless draw at relegation-threatened Sunderland, Petr Cech kept another clean sheet at home to Norwich – a game won by Danny Welbeck's second-half goal. But the Premier League title was now mathematically out of reach and Arsenal went into May third in the table.

RESULTS

Sat 2	Watford	H	4-0	Alexis, Iwobi, Bellerin, Walcott	Premier League
Sat 9	West Ham United	A	3-3	Ozil, Alexis, Koscielny	Premier League
Sun 17	Crystal Palace	H	1-1	Alexis	Premier League
Thu 21	West Brom	H	2-0	Alexis 2	Premier League
Sun 24	Sunderland	A	0-0		Premier League
Sat 30	Norwich City	H	1-0	Welbeck	Premier League

STATS AND FACTS
2-0 was the most common scoreline, recorded seven times

ARSENAL.COM PLAYER OF THE MONTH: MOHAMED ELNENY

Season in Review

MAY

THE GUNNERS TWICE CAME FROM BEHIND to earn a draw away to Manchester City, and virtually seal Champions League qualification for the 19th consecutive season. Olivier Giroud and Alexis Sanchez struck either side of half-time to secure the point, and ensure Arsenal ended the campaign unbeaten against the rest of the teams in the top four. The Gunners then went into the final game of the season knowing only victory over rock-bottom Aston Villa, coupled with a win for already-relegated Newcastle against Tottenham, would be enough to finish second. On a dramatic afternoon, that's exactly what happened.

Newcastle triumphed 5-1 while Giroud scored a hat-trick in Arsenal's 4-0 win at Emirates Stadium. Petr Cech's clean sheet earned him the Premier League Golden Glove award as Arsenal celebrated their highest finish of the Emirates Stadium era. In an emotional send off, Mikel Arteta and Tomas Rosicky both called time on their Arsenal careers at the final whistle.

RESULTS

Sun 8	Manchester City	A	2-2	Giroud, Alexis	Premier League
Sun 15	Aston Villa	H	4-0	Giroud 3, Bunn (og)	Premier League

ARSENAL.COM PLAYER OF THE SEASON: MESUT OZIL

OLIVIER STATS AND FACTS
Giroud was the top scorer (24)

DID YOU KNOW?

Some facts and figures from Arsenal's Premier League campaign:

Arsenal hit the woodwork more than any other side (21 times).

Arsenal's passing accuracy (84%) was the best in the league.

No team kept more clean sheets than Arsenal (18).

Olivier Giroud scored the most headed goals in the league (7).

Mesut Ozil had more assists than any other player in the league (19).

Mesut also created the most goalscoring chances in the league (146).

Arsenal completed more dribbles than any other side in the league (486).

Arsenal took more touches of the ball than any other side (29,337).

GAME	LEAGUE POSITION
1	20
2	11
3	9
4	5
5	3
6	5
7	4
8	2
9	2
10	1
11	2
12	2
13	4
14	4
15	2
16	1
17	2
18	1
19	1
20	1
21	1

GAME	LEAGUE POSITION
22	1
23	3
24	4
25	3
26	2
27	3
28	3
29	3
30	3
31	3
32	3
33	4
34	3
35	4
36	3
37	3
38	2

Mesut Özil

THERE WAS AN OVERWHELMING WINNER OF ARSENAL'S PLAYER OF THE SEASON AWARD.

Mesut Özil was the star of the show throughout the campaign for the Gunners, scoring eight times in all competitions and adding an incredible 20 assists. All but one of those assists came in the league, making him comfortably the most creative player in English football last season.

In fact he was just one away from equaling Thierry Henry's record for most assists ever in a Premier League season.

The German playmaker did break one record though – in November 2015 he became the first player ever to contribute assists in seven consecutive Premier League matches.

The run started with a clipped pass for Alexis Sanchez to score in the 5-2 win away to Leicester City. Özil then turned in a virtuoso display in the next match – a 3-0 win over Manchester United – before he set up two more goals in the win at Watford. After creating for Olivier Giroud to score at home to Everton, a couple more assists followed against Swansea.

A pinpoint cross for Kieran Gibbs's crucial late equaliser against Tottenham was next, before the ninth assist in seven games arrived – Özil floated in a perfect free-kick for Giroud to head home at West Brom.

By the end of 2015, Mesut had racked up an incredible 16 assists, and he'd undoubtedly been the outstanding performer during the first half of that Premier League season.

His 20th assist came on the final day, laying on another goal for Giroud. In fact Giroud benefitted most often from Özil's assists in 2015/16. The Frenchman gobbled up seven of the chances Özil created; Alexis Sanchez and Danny Welbeck netted three each.

In all Özil created 146 goalscoring chances in the Premier League last term, 27 more than any other player. It led to him being shortlisted as PFA Player of the Season.

Özil's creativity and inventiveness have become an instrumental part of Arsenal's game since he arrived at the club from Real Madrid in 2013. In the past three years he's gone from strength to strength in English football, and passed the 100-game landmark for the Gunners last season. A World Cup winner in 2014, and with an impressive Euro 2016 behind him, it looks as though Özil could be in the mood to break more records this season as well.

MESUT ÖZIL'S PREMIER LEAGUE STATS 2015/16

Games	35
Minutes played	3,047
Goals	6
Assists	19
Shots on target	20
Hit woodwork	3
Chances created	146
Successful passes	1,964
Passing accuracy	86%
Passing accuracy in opposition half	85%
Touches	2,963
Tackles won	27
Fouls conceded	20
Fouls won	43
Yellow cards	4
Offsides	15

...Assist King

MOST PL ASSISTS FOR ARSENAL PER SEASON

1999/2000	Dennis Bergkamp	9
2000/01	Thierry Henry	9
2001/02	Robert Pires	15
2002/03	Thierry Henry	20
2003/04	Robert Pires	8
2004/05	Thierry Henry	14
2005/06	Jose Antonio Reyes	10
2006/07	Cesc Fabregas	11
2007/08	Cesc Fabregas	17
2008/09	Robin van Persie	10
2009/10	Cesc Fabregas	13
2010/11	Cesc Fabregas, Andrey Arshavin	11
2011/12	Alex Song	11
2012/13	Santi Cazorla	11
2013/14	Mesut Ozil	9
2014/15	Santi Cazorla	11
2015/16	Mesut Ozil	19

ALL-TIME PREMIER LEAGUE ASSISTS FOR ARSENAL

	Player	Assists
1	Dennis Bergkamp	94
2	Thierry Henry	74
3	Cesc Fabregas	70
4	Theo Walcott	41
5	Robert Pires	41
6	Robin van Persie	39
7 =	Mesut Ozil	33
7 =	Santi Cazorla	33
7 =	Patrick Vieira	33
8	Aaron Ramsey	28

Alex Oxlade-Chamberlain's Dream XI

WE ASKED OUR PLAYERS TO BE MANAGER FOR A DAY, AND CHOOSE THEIR ULTIMATE XI.

GOALKEEPER
PETR CECH
His positioning and shot stopping is the best I've ever seen.

RIGHT BACK
HECTOR BELLERIN
I train against him and his pace means he is so hard to get behind.

CENTRE BACK
JOHN TERRY
He has amazing experience and his positioning is really good.

CENTRE BACK
LAURENT KOSCIELNY
I think he's the best centre back in the Premier League.

LEFT BACK
ASHLEY COLE
Going forward he brought a lot to the table. He was quick, good on the ball, could dribble and scored a few goals.

CENTRE MIDFIELD
STEVEN GERRARD
He can run with the ball, drive through midfield and his range of passing and will to win was amazing.

NUMBER 10
MESUT OZIL
His vision and ability to pick a clever pass is the best I've seen.

CENTRE MIDFIELD
SANTI CAZORLA
Santi is a magician – he's equally good with his right or left foot.

CENTRE FORWARD
ROBIN VAN PERSIE
His first touch was one of the best I've seen.

CENTRE FORWARD
WAYNE ROONEY
He can score from anywhere, and also drop into midfield to play from deeper.

CENTRE FORWARD
THIERRY HENRY
He's the best I've ever seen in the Premier League for sure.

Stat Attack

ARSENAL IN THE PREMIER LEAGUE
All the stats and facts from Arsenal's Premier League history

- 3 LEAGUE TITLES
- 1,747 TOTAL POINTS
- 924 GAMES PLAYED
- 502 GAMES WON
- 1,621 GOALS SCORED (911 RIGHT FOOT, 439 LEFT FOOT, 219 HEADERS, 52 OTHERS)
- 367 CLEAN SHEETS
- 179 PLAYERS
- 107 GOALSCORERS

HAT-TRICK SCORERS

Thierry Henry	8	Ian Wright	5	Emmanuel Adebayor	3	Robin van Persie	3
Theo Walcott	3	Kevin Campbell	2	Nicolas Anelka	1	Andrey Arshavin	1
Dennis Bergkamp	1	Santi Cazorla	1	Olivier Giroud	1	Kanu	1
Freddie Ljungberg	1	Marc Overmars	1	Ray Parlour	1	Jermaine Pennant	1
Robert Pires	1	Alexis Sanchez	1	Sylvain Wiltord	1		

SEASON BY SEASON FINISHING POSITIONS

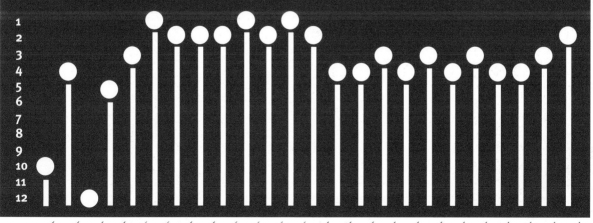

1992/93 1993/94 1994/95 1995/96 1996/97 1997/98 1998/99 1999/00 2000/01 2001/02 2002/03 2003/04 2004/05 2005/06 2006/07 2007/08 2008/09 2009/10 2010/11 2011/12 2012/13 2013/14 2014/15 2015/16

Social Club

Club ... Soc

DO YOU FOLLOW OUR PLAYERS ON SOCIAL MEDIA?

@ALEXIS_OFFICIA1 ON INSTAGRAM
Alexis posted this pic after winning the Copa America for the second year running with Chile.

@PETRCECH ON TWITTER
Petr's wife baked him a 'trophy' for breaking the Premier League clean sheet record!

@THEOWALCOTT ON TWITTER
Theo posted a flashback to his first season at Arsenal.

@_OLIVIERGIROUD_ ON TWITTER
Olivier with France national team mates at Euro 2016.

@M10_OFFICIAL ON INSTAGRAM
Mesut thanks the fans for voting him Arsenal Player of the Season.

Club Social

Here's a taste of what our players get up to on Twitter and Instagram.

@AARONRAMSEY ON INSTAGRAM
Aaron and his son take time out at Emirates at the end of the season.

@ALEXOXCHAMBERLAIN ON INSTAGRAM
Behind the scenes on a night out with Alex's team-mates.

@GRANITXHAKA ON INSTAGRAM
Granit is proud to show his Arsenal colours.

@JACKWILSHERE ON TWITTER
Jack models Ray Parlour's vintage shirt for a feature in the Arsenal programme.

@HECTORBELLERIN ON TWITTER
Hector and Alex are ready to try their hand at commentating.

Stat Attack

Top fives in the Premier League last season

Passes Completed

Player	Passes
Mesut Ozil	1,964
Aaron Ramsey	1,855
Nacho Monreal	1,576
Laurent Koscielny	1,471
Hector Bellerin	1,446

Goals

Player	Goals
Olivier Giroud	16
Alexis Sanchez	13
Mesut Ozil	6
Aaron Ramsey	5
Theo Walcott	5

Assists

Player	Assists
Mesut Ozil	19
Olivier Giroud	6
Hector Bellerin	5
Aaron Ramsey	4
Alexis Sanchez	4

Shots on Target

Olivier Giroud	43
Hector Bellerin	38
Theo Walcott	22
Aaron Ramsey	21
Mesut Ozil	20

Touches

Player	Touches
Mesut Ozil	2,963
Aaron Ramsey	2,774
Nacho Monreal	2,759
Hector Bellerin	2,613
Laurent Koscielny	2,217

Dribbles Completed

Alexis Sanchez	100
Hector Bellerin	62
Mesut Ozil	46
Aaron Ramsey	39
Santi Cazorla	37

Interceptions

Player	Interceptions	Player	Interceptions
Laurent Koscielny	126	Nacho Monreal	105
Francis Coquelin	76	Hector Bellerin	66
		Gabriel	61

Tackles Won

Aaron Ramsey	59
Francis Coquelin	57
Nacho Monreal	56
Hector Bellerin	47
Alexis Sanchez	30

Minutes Played

Nacho Monreal	3,248
Hector Bellerin	3,240
Petr Cech	3,060
Mesut Ozil	3,047
Laurent Koscielny	2,846

Spot the Ball

Answer on p.61

Best of the Best

WE ASKED THE ARSENAL STARS FOR THEIR BEST...

Aaron Ramsey celebrates after scoring in the FA Cup Final.

MOMENT IN FOOTBALL

AARON RAMSEY
My best moment was either scoring the winner in the FA Cup final or captaining my country for the first time.

PETR CECH
For me it's definitely winning the Champions League, it's the ultimate prize. I've won the Premier League, I've won the cups, but this is one trophy that you always dream about.

FRANCIS COQUELIN
I would say the 2015 FA Cup final. It was a great moment, as was when I signed for Arsenal.

AWAY GROUND

LAURENT KOSCIELNY
I like the Etihad Stadium because it's a nice new stadium, the dressing rooms are nice, the fans are good, and also we've had some great results there so that gives you good memories.

FRANCIS COQUELIN
Well I would love to play at Marseille, because it has been completely rebuilt. It is 60,000 now. In the Premier League I would say Old Trafford and of course Wembley is unbelievable.

AARON RAMSEY
I like the old stadiums, like Anfield, and I also like Dortmund.

Etihad Stadium

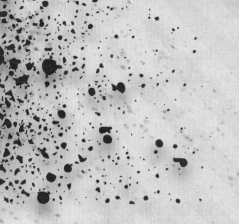

GOAL CELEBRATION

DANNY WELBECK
I've seen loads on YouTube. In the Premier League I thought Wayne Rooney's one when he did the punch and knock out was quite funny after the week he'd been through!

FRANCIS COQUELIN
In the Africa Cup of Nations, I love the goalie who plays for Congo, Robert Kidiaba. He does the crazy celebration where he sits down and dances.

PETR CECH
Remember that Icelandic team from a few years ago? When they pretended to have a fishing rod and they caught one of the players. They had plenty of funny celebrations, it looked like they spent a lot of time working on them!

SINGER IN THE SQUAD

LAURENT KOSCIELNY
It's either Alex Oxlade-Chamberlain or Calum Chambers, they seem to enjoy doing it anyway. They are young and they like rap, things like that. They are usually the first to sing along when we put some music on in the dressing room.

AARON RAMSEY
Chambo fancies himself as a singer so I'll choose him.

CALUM CHAMBERS
Maybe me, if I properly went at it in the studio, I have quite a soothing voice. I think I could do quite well, but I need would some lessons first!

WEATHER FOR FOOTBALL

CALUM CHAMBERS
A shower just before the game so the pitch is nice and wet, then the sun comes out in time for kick off. Wet pitch but sunny weather.

FRANCIS COQUELIN
Typical English weather, a bit of rain, not too hot. It's better for sliding tackles.

PER MERTESACKER
When it's just rained, but it's stopped before the game. I like the roughness and the atmosphere that comes with the rain, you can get a good slide tackle in.

Best of the Best

WE ASKED THE ARSENAL STARS FOR THEIR BEST...

England Rugby

OTHER SPORT TO WATCH

AARON RAMSEY
It's rugby, I love watching that, and I like watching golf too.

CALUM CHAMBERS
I like NFL. When they come to London I try to get to the games. I don't have a favourite team, I don't follow it that closely, but we used to play a bit at school and I just like the sport.

DANNY WELBECK
I probably watched about 90 per cent of the Rugby World Cup in 2015. I was injured the whole time so I watched game after game!

TEAM-MATE TO BE PRIME MINISTER

CALUM CHAMBERS
I would say Flamini, he is always busy. He is always on his phone talking business so he would make a good Prime Minister.

AARON RAMSEY
Per Mertesacker would do a good job.

DANNY WELBECK
I've played with a lot of leaders, but I don't think any of them would make a good Prime Minister! That's a really hard one, but I'll have to go for Per Mertesacker.

Per Mertesacker

Olivier Giroud

DRESSED TEAM-MATE

PER MERTESACKER
Flamini. Sometimes when he has a business meeting after training he will be very smart. He looks very stylish in his suits.

AARON RAMSEY
It's got to be Olivier Giroud for that.

CALUM CHAMBERS
Hector. He comes in some outrageous stuff, but he really does make an effort some days so probably him. He has the best style.

CAR IN THE ARSENAL CAR PARK

AARON RAMSEY
Let's go for Theo Walcott's Mercedes SLS.

FRANCIS COQUELIN
That's Theo's, he loves his cars. From the first day I arrived here, he's always had some crazy cars.

CALUM CHAMBERS
Mesut has a nice car – it's a Lamborghini, very nice.

Mercedes SLS

500 Premier

ARSENAL RACKED UP THEIR 500TH ALL-TIME PREMIER LEAGUE WIN DURING THE 2015/16 SEASON.

ARSENAL 4, EVERTON 0
HIGHBURY, MAY 3, 1998

Arsène Wenger's first league title was celebrated in sensational fashion, with captain Tony Adams providing the coup de grace.

A superb run of form from the turn of the year had put Arsenal within touching distance of the title in Wenger's first full season in north London. A win over Everton would seal the crown, and a Slaven Bilic own goal on just four minutes set them on the way. Marc Overmars scored two fine breakaway goals either side of half-time to start the celebrations. The best was yet to come though. In the final moments, Steve Bould sent a ball over the top and Adams, of all people, found himself bearing down on goal. He lashed home left-footed in front of the North Bank to win the league with two games to spare.

Arsenal: Seaman, Dixon, Winterburn, Keown, Adams, Parlour, Vieira, Petit (Platt), Overmars, Anelka (Wright), Wreh (Bould).

ARSENAL 7, EVERTON 0
HIGHBURY, MAY 11, 2005

The last time Arsenal ever wore the famous red and white strip at Highbury resulted in a 7-0 hammering of Everton.

The visitors had just confirmed fourth place in the league, and a first ever qualification for the Champions League, but they were up against a rampant Gunners, who were 2-0 up after 12 minutes through Robin van Persie and Robert Pires. Patrick Vieira made it 3-0 before Thierry Henry was introduced at half-time, having been rested with the FA Cup final just 10 days away. But for once Henry was overshadowed as further goals came from Pires again, Edu (on his last Highbury outing), Dennis Bergkamp (who also made three assists) and Mathieu Flamini (his first for the Gunners). It was the biggest win of Arsène Wenger's reign.

Arsenal: Lehmann, Lauren, Campbell, Senderos, Cole, Vieira (Flamini), Edu, Pires (Fabregas), Bergkamp, van Persie (Henry), Reyes.

MANCHESTER UNITED 0, ARSENAL 1
OLD TRAFFORD, MAY 8, 2002

Arsenal secured the league title at the home of the reigning champions, thanks to Sylvain Wiltord's second half winner.

Four days after winning the FA Cup, Arsenal needed just a point from the encounter at Old Trafford to earn a 12th title, but they deservedly took all three. Freddie Ljungberg, who had scored six times in the previous six matches to push Arsenal to the brink of the double, forced his way through on goal again in the 56th minute. Fabien Barthez parried the effort but only to Wiltord, who swept home with his left foot. David Seaman remained untroubled at the other end as Arsenal capped a remarkable season in suitable fashion, despite top scorer Thierry Henry – as well as skipper Tony Adams – both being absent through injury.

Arsenal: Seaman, Lauren, Keown, Campbell, Cole, Ljungberg, Parlour, Vieira, Edu, Wiltord, Kanu (Dixon).

Sol Campbell, Patrick Vieira and Ashley Cole celebrate victory over Manchester United

Theo Walcott celebrates scoring his 2nd goal against Tottenham

League wins

HERE WE REMEMBER FIVE CLASSICS...

 ARSENAL 2, LEICESTER CITY 1
HIGHBURY, MAY 15, 2004

Arsenal's status as the first unbeaten champions in the modern era was confirmed with a comeback win over Leicester at Highbury.

Already crowned champions, the Gunners had just one remaining objective in the 38th and final league game of 2003/04 – to not lose and hence become the first 'invincibles' since Preston North End achieved the feat in the 22-game 1888/89 season. Former Gunner Paul Dickov threatened to ruin the party when he headed home in the first half, but Arsenal duly turned the game around in the second half. Thierry Henry converted a 46th-minute penalty and captain Patrick Vieira sealed the win, running on to Dennis Bergkamp's throughball, to make history.

Arsenal: Lehmann, Lauren, Toure, Campbell, Cole, Ljungberg (Keown), Gilberto, Vieira, Pires (Edu), Bergkamp (Reyes), Henry.

 ARSENAL 5, TOTTENHAM HOTSPUR 2
EMIRATES STADIUM, FEBRUARY 26, 2012

Arsenal went into the derby match 10 points behind their rivals, with just 13 games of the season remaining, but they dismantled Spurs with a stunning display.

The pressure was well and truly on when Louis Saha netted after four minutes and ex-Gunner Emmanuel Adebayor doubled the lead on 34 minutes.

Despite their deficit, Arsenal refused to buckle and Bacary Sagna's firm header gave them hope of a comeback five minutes before half time. Moments later a magical Robin van Persie strike restored parity. The hosts' dominance continued after the restart and the excellent Tomas Rosicky completed a dramatic turnaround when he prodded in on 51 minutes. The spotlight then fell on Theo Walcott, who scored two fine goals in three minutes, and the Gunners would go on to finish above their neighbours once again.

Arsenal: Szczesny, Sagna, Vermaelen, Koscielny, Gibbs (Jenkinson), Rosicky, Arteta, Walcott (Oxlade-Chamberlain), Song, Benayoun (Gervinho), van Persie.

Unbeaten league champions in 2004

PREMIER LEAGUE WINS PER SEASON

Season	Wins	Season	Wins
1992/93	15	2004/05	25
1993/94	18	2005/06	20
1994/95	13	2006/07	19
1995/96	17	2007/08	24
1996/97	19	2008/09	20
1997/98	23	2009/10	23
1998/99	22	2010/11	19
1999/2000	22	2011/12	21
2000/01	20	2012/13	21
2001/02	26	2013/14	24
2002/03	23	2014/15	22
2003/04	26	2015/16	20

Laurent Koscielny's Dream XI

We asked our players to be manager for a day, and choose their ultimate XI.

GOALKEEPER
FABIEN BARTHEZ
He was amazing and he won everything as a player.

RIGHT BACK
CAFU
He was unbelievable, going from box to box was no problem for him.

CENTRE BACK
ALESSANDRO NESTA
He played really well on the ball and was a great defender.

CENTRE BACK
CARLES PUYOL
He was the emblem of Barcelona during his career.

LEFT BACK
ROBERTO CARLOS
I remember the free-kick he scored against France when he curled it past the wall.

RIGHT WING
DAVID BECKHAM
He could always deliver the ball wherever he wanted for the striker.

CENTRE MIDFIELD
MARCO VERRATTI
He has unbelievable technique and he takes some risks.

CENTRE MIDFIELD
XAVI
He won everything with his club and the national team.

LEFT WING
CHRIS WADDLE
He was my idol when he played for Marseille.

NUMBER 10
ZINEDINE ZIDANE
For a Frenchman he's the king.

STRIKER
THIERRY HENRY
He was amazing for the France national team and of course for Arsenal.

Match the 49ers!

EACH QUESTION IS WORTH SEVEN GAMES – REMAIN UNBEATEN THROUGHOUT THE QUIZ AND YOU CAN MATCH THE FAMOUS 49ERS – THE ARSENAL SIDE WHO WENT A RECORD 49 LEAGUE GAMES UNDEFEATED BETWEEN MAY 2003 AND OCTOBER 2004.

1 True or False? Arsenal scored two hat-tricks in the very first game of the 49-game unbeaten run?

2 With 39 goals, who was Arsenal's top scorer during the run?

3 Name this player, who played 23 times during the unbeaten run.

4 What was the score in game number 36, in which Arsenal secured the league title against Tottenham at White Hart Lane?

6 This was game number 42 of the run, equaling the old record. Who did Arsenal beat 5-3 in this match?

5 Who scored the winning goal against Leicester on the last day of 2003/04, to complete the 'Invincibles' season?

7 How many of the 49 games did Arsenal win? Was it 30, 36 or 42?

Aaron Ramsey's Dream XI

WE ASKED OUR PLAYERS TO BE MANAGER FOR A DAY, AND CHOOSE THEIR ULTIMATE XI.

GOALKEEPER
PETR CECH
He's got the record for most clean sheets in the Premier League.

RIGHT BACK
PHILIPP LAHM
A sensational player who has won many trophies.

CENTRE BACK
RIO FERDINAND
A great centre back who can get the ball down and play from the back.

CENTRE BACK
FABIO CANNAVARO
Fabio is a similar type of player to Rio.

LEFT BACK
ROBERTO CARLOS
He had a thunderbolt of a strike on him.

CENTRE MIDFIELD
ZINEDINE ZIDANE
A world-class player, one of my favourite players of all time.

CENTRE MIDFIELD
STEVEN GERRARD
He's an all-round complete midfielder.

CENTRE MIDFIELD
ANDRES INIESTA
He's won everything there is to win in the game.

CENTRE FORWARD
LIONEL MESSI
For me he's probably the greatest player

CENTRE FORWARD
CRISTIANO RONALDO
What he has achieved throughout his

CENTRE FORWARD
THIERRY HENRY
He's obviously an Arsenal legend.

Emirates Stadium Quiz

HOW MUCH DO YOU KNOW ABOUT THE HOME OF FOOTBALL?

1. WHO SCORED ARSENAL'S FIRST EVER COMPETITIVE GOAL AT THE STADIUM?

2. IS THE FAMOUS CLOCK SITUATED ON THE NORTH, EAST, WEST OR SOUTH SIDE OF THE STADIUM?

3. WHICH FORMER DEFENDER HAS A STATUE OUTSIDE THE STADIUM?

4. WHICH TEAM DID ARSENAL BEAT 5-2 TWICE AT EMIRATES STADIUM IN 2012?

5. WHICH PLAYER HAS PLAYED THE MOST GAMES AT EMIRATES STADIUM?

6. WHAT IS THE EXACT CAPACITY OF EMIRATES? IS IT 59,009, 60,272 OR 61,765?

7. WHICH NATIONAL TEAM HAS PLAYED SEVEN TIMES AT EMIRATES STADIUM?

8. WHO WON THE EMIRATES CUP IN 2015?

9. TRUE OR FALSE, COLDPLAY ONCE PLAYED A CONCERT AT EMIRATES STADIUM?

10. IN WHICH YEAR DID ARSENAL MOVE TO EMIRATES STADIUM?

11. HOW MANY GIANT SCREENS ARE INSIDE THE STADIUM?

12. ARSENAL'S FIRST FOUR LEAGUE WINS AT EMIRATES STADIUM WERE ALL BY THE SAME SCORELINE. WHAT WAS IT?

Answers on p.61

Arsenal Ladies

A RECORD CROWD OF MORE THAN 32,000 WERE AT WEMBLEY Stadium to witness Arsenal Ladies win an incredible 14th FA Cup, with victory over Chelsea.

England striker Danielle Carter scored the only goal of the game – a cracking strike from a difficult angle – in the first half, and the Gunners held on for the win, despite going into the game as underdogs. It was the first FA Cup success for manager Pedro Martinez Losa, and it's the first time Arsenal have lifted the famous trophy at Wembley Stadium.

But it's far from the first time the club have triumphed in this competition. In fact their tally of 14 wins (from 15 finals) is six more than the second most successful side: Southampton.

After the final whistle captain Alex Scott went up to lift the cup – the seventh time in her career she had done so in Arsenal colours.

THEY SAID:

CASEY STONEY
"I can't take the smile off my face. I'm just trying to soak up every minute because it's not every day you get to play at Wembley in an FA Cup final. I have to say we deserved it today – credit to our squad, our team, our players out there and the manager for getting his tactics right. I think we were spot on and Chelsea didn't know what hit them."

DANIELLE CARTER
"It's out of this world. It's the first time we've won it at Wembley but it's my fourth time since I've been at Arsenal. Each time gets better and better. I don't think I've ever scored a more important goal."

PEDRO MARTINEZ LOSA
"I hope the fans felt proud. I have to say thank you very much to them. I hope they enjoyed the game, I hope we can make them proud in the future."

WINNERS

THE SSE WOMEN'S FA CUP FINAL

ARSENAL LADIES FA CUP WINS

1993	Arsenal 3-0 Doncaster Belles
1995	Arsenal 3-2 Liverpool
1998	Arsenal 3-2 Croydon
1999	Arsenal 2-0 Southampton Saints
2001	Arsenal 1-0 Fulham
2004	Arsenal 3-0 Charlton Athletic
2006	Arsenal 5-0 Leeds United
2007	Arsenal 4-1 Charlton Athletic
2008	Arsenal 4-1 Leeds United
2009	Arsenal 2-1 Sunderland
2011	Arsenal 2-0 Bristol Academy
2013	Arsenal 3-0 Bristol Academy
2014	Arsenal 2-0 Everton
2016	Arsenal 1-0 Chelsea

Player Profiles

GOALKEEPERS

13

DAVID OSPINA

Agile shot-stopper David impressed when called upon last season, playing 12 times in all competitions and keeping four clean sheets. The Colombian joined from French side Nice in 2014, and ended his first season with an FA Cup winner's medal. In the summer David starred for his country at the Copa America, and was the hero as Colombia won a penalty shoot-out against Peru in the quarter-final.

BORN:
MEDELLIN, COLOMBIA, AUG 31, 1988

JOINED ARSENAL:
FROM NICE ON JULY 27, 2014

PREVIOUS CLUBS:
ATLETICO NACIONAL, NICE

ARSENAL DEBUT:
v SOUTHAMPTON (H) LEAGUE CUP, SEPT 23, 2014

PETR CECH

Experienced keeper Petr enjoyed a fantastic first season at Arsenal, winning the Premier League Golden Glove award for keeping the most clean sheets. He won the Community Shield on his debut against former side Chelsea, to add to the four Premier League titles, four FA Cups and one Champions League trophy he won before joining. The most capped Czech player of all time, Petr appeared at Euro 2016 before retiring from international football.

33

BORN:
PILSEN, CZECH REPUBLIC, MAY 20, 1982

JOINED ARSENAL:
FROM CHELSEA ON JUNE 29, 2015

PREVIOUS CLUBS:
CHMEL BLSANY, SPARTA PRAGUE, RENNES, CHELSEA

ARSENAL DEBUT:
v CHELSEA (N) COMMUNITY SHIELD, AUG 2, 2015

EMILIANO MARTINEZ

26

Highly-rated goalkeeper Emi impressed during a fine spell on loan at Championship side Wolverhampton Wanderers last season. The Argentine stopper had already played for Arsenal in three different competitions, including the Champions League in 2014/15. On his route to the Arsenal first team, the 6ft 4in Argentina youth international enjoyed several loan spells in England, after signing for the Gunners as a teenager in 2010.

BORN:
BUENOS AIRES, ARGENTINA, SEPT 2, 1992

JOINED ARSENAL:
FROM INDEPENDIENTE ON AUG 1, 2010

PREVIOUS CLUBS:
INDEPENDIENTE, OXFORD UNITED (LOAN), SHEFFIELD WEDNESDAY (LOAN), ROTHERHAM UNITED (LOAN), WOLVES (LOAN)

ARSENAL DEBUT:
V COVENTRY CITY (H), LEAGUE CUP, SEPT 26, 2012

DEFENDERS

PER MERTESACKER

The regular skipper in Mikel Arteta's absence last season, Per has taken on the captaincy full time this season. A talisman at the heart of the Arsenal defence, the 6ft 6in German centre half has now played more than 200 times for the club, after joining from Werder Bremen in 2011. An experienced, natural leader who is dominant in the air, Per won the World Cup in 2014, having been a runner-up at the 2008 European Championships.

BORN:
HANNOVER, GERMANY, SEPT 29, 1984

JOINED ARSENAL:
FROM WERDER BREMEN ON AUG 31, 2011

PREVIOUS CLUBS:
HANNOVER 96, WERDER BREMEN

ARSENAL DEBUT:
V SWANSEA CITY (H) LEAGUE, SEPT 10, 2011

04

KIERAN GIBBS

03

Dependable and consistent defender Kieran brought up his 200th appearance for the Arsenal first team last season, having joined the club's youth setup in 2004. Fast and incisive in possession, Kieran loves to advance from defence, drawing upon his experience as a winger from his days in the Arsenal academy. Now an established left back, he has been regularly involved for England since making his senior international debut in 2011.

BORN:
LAMBETH, SEPT 26, 1989

JOINED ARSENAL:
AS A SCHOLAR IN SUMMER 2006

PREVIOUS CLUB:
NORWICH CITY (LOAN)

ARSENAL DEBUT:
V SHEFFIELD UNITED (A) LEAGUE CUP, OCT 31, 2007

GABRIEL

05

A committed, robust defender who is also strong in the air, Gabriel featured regularly throughout his first full season at the club, and claimed his first Gunners goal in the home win over Bournemouth. The Brazilian (also known as Gabriel Paulista) joined from Spanish club Villarreal, after starting his career with Vitoria in his home country. Usually a centre back, though also able to play at full back, he brings strength and a fierce competitive spirit to the back line.

BORN:
SAO PAULO, BRAZIL, NOV 26, 1990

JOINED ARSENAL:
FROM VILLARREAL ON JAN 28, 2015

PREVIOUS CLUBS:
VITORIA, VILLARREAL

ARSENAL DEBUT:
v MIDDLESBROUGH (H) FA CUP, FEB 15, 2015

LAURENT KOSCIELNY

06

A valuable part of the Arsenal defence since joining in 2010, Laurent is among the leading defenders in world football. As well as being composed and calm on the ball, Laurent reads the game superbly, and has a welcome habit of scoring important goals. Fast, strong and dominant in the duels, the France international played all seven games at Euro 2016, helping his country reach the final on home soil.

BORN:
TULLE, FRANCE, SEPT 10, 1985

JOINED ARSENAL:
FROM LORIENT ON JULY 2, 2010

PREVIOUS CLUBS:
GUINGAMP, TOURS, LORIENT

ARSENAL DEBUT:
v LIVERPOOL (A) LEAGUE, AUG 15, 2010

NACHO MONREAL

18

Undoubtedly one of Arsenal's most consistent players in recent years, the 2015/16 season was perhaps Nacho's best yet. The Pamplona-born left back was virtually ever-present, missing only one Premier League match. A full Spain international, Nacho joined from Malaga, where he was a team-mate of Santi Cazorla and has now played more than 100 times for the Gunners, impressing with his expert positioning and calmness under pressure.

BORN:
PAMPLONA, SPAIN, FEB 26, 1986

JOINED ARSENAL:
FROM MALAGA ON JAN 31, 2013

PREVIOUS CLUBS:
OSASUNA, MALAGA

ARSENAL DEBUT:
v STOKE CITY (H) LEAGUE, FEB 2, 2013

MATHIEU DEBUCHY

02

Experienced right back Mathieu played much of his football on loan to Ligue 1 side Bordeaux last term. He had started the season with Arsenal, playing seven times to add to the 15 appearances he made during his debut campaign. The attack-minded full back signed from Newcastle in 2014, after playing more than 300 times for Lille earlier in his career. A France international who starred at Euro 2012 and the 2014 World Cup, he won the French league and cup double in 2010/11.

BORN:
FRETIN, FRANCE, JULY 29, 1985

JOINED ARSENAL:
FROM NEWCASTLE UTD ON JULY 17, 2014

PREVIOUS CLUBS:
LILLE, NEWCASTLE UTD, BORDEAUX (LOAN)

ARSENAL DEBUT:
v MANCHESTER CITY (N) COMMUNITY SHIELD, AUG 10, 2014

CARL JENKINSON

25

Hard-working right back Carl featured 20 times on loan for West Ham last season, before sustaining a cruciate ligament injury. A boyhood Gunners fan, Carl joined the club from Charlton in 2012. He scored once in 57 appearances for Arsenal, and helped the team lift the FA Cup in 2014, before his first loan spell with West Ham. A senior England international since 2012, Carl has also been an Under-21s regular for the Three Lions, having represented Finland at youth level earlier in his career.

BORN:
HARLOW, FEB 8, 1992

JOINED ARSENAL:
FROM CHARLTON ATHLETIC ON JUNE 8, 2011

PREVIOUS CLUBS:
CHARLTON ATHLETIC, EASTBOURNE BOROUGH (LOAN), WELLING UTD (LOAN), WEST HAM UTD (LOAN)

ARSENAL DEBUT:
v UDINESE (H) CHAMPIONS LEAGUE, AUG 16, 2011

HECTOR BELLERIN

24

Pacey, attacking young right back Hector was a regular in the Arsenal defence last season, impressing with his frequent bursts forward and incisive passing. Only Mesut Ozil made more starts than Hector last term, and he was third in the assists charts with nine in all competitions. He joined the Arsenal academy from Barcelona at the age of 16 and is now a full Spain international, having won his first senior cap just before Euro 2016.

BORN:
BARCELONA, SPAIN, MAR 19, 1995

JOINED ARSENAL:
AS A SCHOLAR IN SUMMER 2011

PREVIOUS CLUB:
WATFORD (LOAN)

ARSENAL DEBUT:
v WEST BROM (A) LEAGUE CUP, SEPT 25, 2013

MIDFIELDERS

08

AARON RAMSEY

Long-serving and influential midfielder Aaron enjoyed another impressive season. The all-round midfielder is strong in the tackle, has tremendous stamina, an eye for a pass and also weighs in with his fair share of goals. Scorer of the winning goal in the 2014 FA Cup final, he suffered a serious leg injury in early 2010, but recovered to make more than 250 appearances for the club so far. He was in sensational form for Wales at Euro 2016, claiming four assists in the tournament.

BORN:
CAERPHILLY, WALES, DEC 26, 1990

JOINED ARSENAL:
FROM CARDIFF CITY ON JUNE 13, 2008

PREVIOUS CLUBS:
CARDIFF CITY, NOTTINGHAM FOREST (LOAN), CARDIFF CITY (LOA

ARSENAL DEBUT:
v FC TWENTE (A) CHAMPIONS LEAGUE, AUG 13, 2008

EFF REINE-ADELAIDE

Pacey winger Jeff was promoted to the first-team squad last summer after an impressive debut season in London. Signed from RC Lens in 2015, the Frenchman made his senior debut in the home FA Cup win over Sunderland, a few days before his 18th birthday. He featured again in the 4-0 FA Cup win at Hull, but it was at youth level where he played the majority of his football last term. Technically gifted, creative and quick, the exciting France youth international has all the qualities to succeed in a number of roles in midfield or attack, though he generally plays on the wing.

BORN:
CHAMPIGNY-SUR-MARNE, FRANCE, JAN 17, 1998

JOINED ARSENAL:
FROM RC LENS ON JULY 1, 2015

PREVIOUS CLUB:
RC LENS

ARSENAL DEBUT:
v SUNDERLAND (H) FA CUP, JAN 9, 2016

31

11

MESUT OZIL

Playmaker Mesut was at his creative best last season, racking up an incredible 20 assists in all competitions. Unquestionably one of the star performers in the Premier League, he was nominated for the PFA Player of the Year and duly took the club award for Player of the Season. One of the world's best in the number 10 position, he has an outstanding ability to carve out chances with his vision and guile. The four-time Germany Player of the Year an 2014 World Cup winner starred at Euro 2016 in the summer.

BORN:
GELSENKIRCHEN, GERMANY, OCT 15, 1988

JOINED ARSENAL:
FROM REAL MADRID ON SEPT 2, 2013

PREVIOUS CLUBS:
SCHALKE, WERDER BREMEN, REAL MADRID

ARSENAL DEBUT:
v SUNDERLAND (A) LEAGUE, SEPT 14, 2013

Santi Cazorla

19

One of the league's most technically-gifted players, Santi has become an integral part of the squad since arriving from Malaga in 2012. The playmaker started his Arsenal career operating behind the striker, but now generally plays in a more withdrawn position, orchestrating the play from deep. Injury restricted him to 15 Premier League appearances last season, but he still created more chances than all but two (Mesut Ozil and Alexis) of his team-mates (38). An experienced Spain international, he won the European Championships in 2008 and 2012.

BORN:
LLANERA, SPAIN, DEC 13, 1984

JOINED ARSENAL:
FROM MALAGA ON AUG 7, 2012

PREVIOUS CLUBS:
VILLARREAL, VILLARREAL B, RECREATIVO HUELVA, MALAGA

ARSENAL DEBUT:
V SUNDERLAND (H) LEAGUE, AUG 18, 2012

Francis Coquelin

An aggressive, indefatigable central midfielder and intelligent reader of the game, Francis has proved his worth to Arsenal over the past two campaigns, and now has more than 100 appearances to his name. As feisty and tenacious as ever, Francis added another element to his game in 2015/16, combining his tough-tackling approach with more incisive passing and surging forward runs. An FA Youth Cup winner in 2009, he had loan spells in France, Germany and England before cementing his place in the team in late 2014.

34

BORN:
LAVAL, FRANCE, MAY 13, 1991

JOINED ARSENAL:
FROM LAVAL ON JULY 22, 2008

PREVIOUS CLUBS:
LAVAL, LORIENT (LOAN), FREIBERG (LOAN), CHARLTON ATHLETIC (LOAN)

ARSENAL DEBUT:
V SHEFFIELD UNITED (H) LEAGUE CUP, SEPT 23, 2008

Mohamed Elneny

35

Mohamed capped a fine debut campaign at Arsenal by winning the club's Goal of the Season award for his strike against Barcelona at the Nou Camp. The classy central midfielder regularly covers the most ground of any Arsenal player when named in the starting line up. Capable of shielding the back four or getting forward in a box-to-box role, energetic Mohamed is a full Egypt international who won three successive Swiss league titles with previous club FC Basel.

BORN:
EL-MAHALLA EL-KUBRA, EGYPT, JULY 11, 1992

JOINED ARSENAL:
FROM BASEL ON JAN 14, 2016

PREVIOUS CLUBS:
EL MOKAWLOON, BASEL

ARSENAL DEBUT:
V BURNLEY (H) FA CUP, JAN 30, 2016

FORWARDS

ALEXIS SANCHEZ

07

Explosive forward Alexis proved his undoubted worth to Arsenal again last season. The all-action, energetic front man, who can play wide or in a more central attacking position, scored 17 goals and contributed 11 assists in all competitions. It followed an incredible first season in England, during which he scored a screamer in the FA Cup final and was named PFA Fans' Player of the Season. He was player of the tournament as he helped Chile win the 2016 Copa America, earning his 100th cap in the process.

BORN:
TOCOPILLA, CHILE, DEC 19, 1988

JOINED ARSENAL:
FROM BARCELONA ON JULY 10, 2014

PREVIOUS CLUBS:
COBRELOA, COLO COLO, RIVER PLATE, UDINESE, BARCELONA

ARSENAL DEBUT:
V MAN CITY (N) COMMUNITY SHIELD, AUG 10, 2014

OLIVIER GIROUD

12

Averaging virtually a goal every two games, Olivier was Arsenal's top scorer with 24 in all competitions last season. The 6ft 4in France international striker, who links play well and relishes the physical battle with his markers, scored two hat-tricks during the campaign. He took his good form into the European Championships – scoring the first goal of the tournament and netting two more in the knock-out stages as France reached the final in Paris.

BORN:
CHAMBERY, FRANCE, SEPT 30, 1986

JOINED ARSENAL:
FROM MONTPELLIER ON JUNE 26, 2012

PREVIOUS CLUBS:
GRENOBLE, ISTRES (LOAN), TOURS, MONTPELLIER

ARSENAL DEBUT:
V SUNDERLAND (H) LEAGUE, AUG 18, 2012

THEO WALCOTT

14

Theo is the leading appearance maker and goalscorer among the current first-team squad. Usually deployed on the right wing or as a centre-forward, the England international, who celebrated 10 years at the club in January 2016, ended the campaign 15 away from a century for the club. Theo was just 16 when he signed from Southampton, and shortly afterwards he became England's youngest-ever full international.

BORN:
MIDDLESEX, MAR 16, 1989

JOINED ARSENAL:
FROM SOUTHAMPTON ON JAN 20, 2006

PREVIOUS CLUB:
SOUTHAMPTON

ARSENAL DEBUT:
v ASTON VILLA (H) LEAGUE, AUG 19, 2006

ALEX OXLADE-CHAMBERLAIN

15

England international Alex began last season with the winner at Wembley in the Community Shield against Chelsea, and finished it by playing his 100th Premier League match. Usually deployed on the right wing, but also capable of playing in central midfield, Alex is quick, strong and direct, with a natural ability to beat defenders. The former Southampton man, son of former England international Mark Chamberlain, made his own senior international debut while still a teenager.

BORN:
PORTSMOUTH, AUG 15, 1993

JOINED ARSENAL:
FROM SOUTHAMPTON ON AUG 8, 2011

PREVIOUS CLUB:
SOUTHAMPTON

ARSENAL DEBUT:
v MANCHESTER UNITED (A) LEAGUE,
AUG 28, 2011

FORWARDS

17

ALEX IWOBI

Skilful forward Alex cemented his place in the first-team squad during a superb breakthrough campaign. Within the space of a week in March 2016 he made his first Champions League start – against Barcelona at the Nou Camp – then marked his first Premier League start with a goal at Everton. All while still a teenager. Naturally a winger, Alex, who is the nephew of former Nigeria star Jay-Jay Okocha, joined Arsenal aged seven. A former England youth international, he is now a full international for Nigeria.

BORN:
LAGOS, NIGERIA, MAY 3, 1996

JOINED ARSENAL:
AS A SCHOLAR IN SUMMER 2012

ARSENAL DEBUT:
v SHEFFIELD WEDNESDAY (A) LEAGUE CUP, OCT 27, 2015

YAYA SANOGO

France Under-21 forward Yaya gained first-team experience away from north London last term. The 6ft 4in striker was with Ajax in the Netherlands, before being loaned to Championship side Charlton Athletic, where he scored a hat-trick on his first start. A powerful forward, Yaya netted his first competitive Arsenal goal against Borussia Dortmund in 2014, having scored four in the Emirates Cup at the start of that season. Yaya joined from Auxerre, after helping France win the Under-20 World Cup in 2013.

22

BORN:
MASSY, FRANCE, JAN 27, 1993

JOINED ARSENAL:
FROM AUXERRE ON JULY 1, 2013

PREVIOUS CLUBS:
LES ULIS, AUXERRE, CRYSTAL PALACE (LOAN), AJAX (LOAN), CHARLTON ATHLETIC (LOAN)

ARSENAL DEBUT:
v FULHAM (A) LEAGUE, AUG 24, 2013

DANNY WELBECK

23

Athletic forward Danny endured a largely-frustrating second term in north London. The England international missed the first six months of the season due to a knee injury, but he marked his first appearance of the campaign in style, scoring a last-minute winner at home to Leicester City in February. A fast, skilful forward who can play through the middle or out wide, Danny joined from Manchester United, where he won the league title in 2013. He has been prolific for England since making his debut in 2011.

BORN:
MANCHESTER, NOV 26, 1990

JOINED ARSENAL:
FROM MANCHESTER UNITED ON SEPT 2, 2014

PREVIOUS CLUBS:
MANCHESTER UNITED, PRESTON NE (LOAN), SUNDERLAND (LOAN)

ARSENAL DEBUT:
V MAN CITY (H) LEAGUE, SEPT 13, 2014

CHUBA AKPOM

Promising striker Chuba returned to Arsenal last summer after helping Hull City earn promotion from the Championship while on loan. Born in east London, Chuba joined the club's Hale End academy aged six, progressing through the ranks to make his Arsenal debut in September 2013. Having represented England since Under-16 level, he marked his first two Under-21s appearances with goals in the young Lions' European Championship qualifying wins over Kazakhstan and Switzerland last season.

32

BORN:
NEWHAM, OCT 9, 1995

JOINED ARSENAL:
AS A SCHOLAR IN SUMMER 2012

PREVIOUS CLUBS:
COVENTRY CITY (LOAN), BRENTFORD (LOAN), NOTTINGHAM FOREST (LOAN), HULL CITY (LOAN)

ARSENAL DEBUT:
V SUNDERLAND (A) LEAGUE, SEPT 14, 2013

New Signings

29

Granit Xhaka

Swiss midfielder Granit became Arsenal's first summer signing when he joined just before Euro 2016, from German side Borussia Monchengladbach. Before playing in Germany the tough, combative central midfielder with an eye for a long pass and a fierce shot, spent 10 years with hometown club Basel. Playing alongside his older brother Taulant, Granit won two Swiss League titles and the Swiss Cup there. A natural leader and seasoned Switzerland international with more than 40 caps, Granit has also tasted success at youth level, winning the 2009 Under-17 World Cup. He made his Gunners debut on the opening day of the season against Liverpool.

BORN:
BASEL, SWITZERLAND, SEPTEMBER 27, 1992

POSITION:
MIDFIELDER

JOINED ARSENAL:
FROM BORUSSIA MONCHENGLADBACH
ON MAY 25, 2016

PREVIOUS CLUBS:
BASEL, BORUSSIA MONCHENGLADBACH

Rob Holding

Promising young defender joined Arsenal from Bolton Wanderers on the eve of the new season. The central defender had been with his childhood club from the age of seven, and rose through the ranks before making his senior debut, aged 19, in August 2015. He soon cemented his place in the side with a string of impressive performances in the Championship, and was named as Bolton's Player of the Season. Last summer he claimed his first international honours too, helping England Under-21s win the Toulon Tournament, shortly before joining the Gunners. Rob then starred in the pre-season tour to America, before making his Arsenal debut on the opening day of the Premier League season.

16

BORN:
TAMESIDE, SEPTEMBER 20, 1995

POSITION:
DEFENDER

JOINED ARSENAL:
FROM BOLTON WANDERERS ON JULY 22, 2016

PREVIOUS CLUBS:
BOLTON WANDERERS, BURY (LOAN)

20

SHKODRAN MUSTAFI

Arsenal's most expensive ever defender, Germany international Shkodran joined from Valencia just before the transfer deadline. The talented central defender had spent two seasons in Spain's La Liga, having previously starred for Sampdoria in Italy. He began his career with Hamburg's youth team, but moved to Everton – aged 17 – in 2009. He played just once for the Toffees though, before leaving for Sampdoria. Shkodran regularly played for Germany's youth sides – representing every age group from under-16 to under-21, before making his senior international debut in 2014. Later that year he helped Germany win the World Cup and he also featured at Euro 2016, scoring in the 2-0 win over Ukraine.

BORN:
BAD HERSFELD, GERMANY, APRIL 17, 1992

POSITION:
DEFENDER

JOINED ARSENAL:
FROM VALENCIA ON AUGUST 30, 2016

PREVIOUS CLUBS:
EVERTON, SAMPDORIA, VALENCIA

LUCAS PEREZ

Versatile frontman Lucas joined Arsenal from Deportivo La Coruna shortly before the transfer deadline, following an impressive season in La Liga. The pacey forward – who can play as a central striker or out wide – scored 17 times during 2015/16, and also contributed 10 assists. A genuinely two-footed, unselfish forward, Lucas had spent two seasons with Deportivo, having joined from Greek side PAOK. Born in the Galician region of Spain, Lucas actually began his senior career with Atletico Madrid's C team, before playing for Rayo Vallecano, then Karpity Lviv in Ukraine. But it was at home-town club Deportivo where powerful forward Lucas really made his name, and he equalled their club record for scoring in successive matches last season.

09

BORN:
LA CORUNA, SPAIN, SEPTEMBER 10, 1988

POSITION:
FORWARD

JOINED ARSENAL:
FROM DEPORTIVO LA CORUNA ON AUGUST 30, 2016

PREVIOUS CLUBS:
ATLETICO MADRID C, RAYO VALLECANO, KARPATY LVIV, DYNAMO KYIV (LOAN), PAOK, DEPORTIVO LA CORUNA

Young Guns

THESE THREE YOUNG MIDFIELDERS ALL MADE THEIR FIRST-TEAM DEBUTS LAST SEASON. HERE'S THE LOWDOWN ON THE LATEST PLAYERS TO EMERGE FROM THE ARSENAL TALENT PRODUCTION LINE.

KRYSTIAN BIELIK

The captain of Arsenal's FA Youth Cup team last season, Krystian enjoyed a cameo appearance in the Capital One Cup, playing the last half-hour in a central midfield role. It was the Pole's long-awaited debut after joining the Gunners, shortly after his 17th birthday, during the winter transfer window in 2015. Arsenal snapped him up from Legia Warsaw, where he had already made an impression in their first team, including playing in the Europa League as a 16 year old. A regular Poland youth international, at 6ft 2in he is an imposing presence as a defensive midfielder, but can also operate at centre half. A constant threat at set pieces, he missed just two games for Arsenal under-21s last season, scoring once.

BORN:
POLAND, JANUARY 4, 1998

ISMAEL BENNACER

Creative midfielder Ismael enjoyed an excellent first season at Arsenal, culminating in his first-team debut against Sheffield Wednesday in the Capital One Cup. The French youngster was brought on after just 19 minutes following Theo Walcott's injury. Although small in stature, Ismael is a feisty competitor, earning the right to orchestrate play in the middle of the park with his excellent passing range. A France youth international at under-18 and under-19 levels, he joined the club from Arles in the summer of 2015, having played at senior level for the French team. Ismael was used for all age groups at Arsenal last term, playing all six games in the FA Youth Cup, and finding the net for both the under-21 and under-19 teams.

BORN:
FRANCE, DECEMBER 1, 1997

GLEN KAMARA

Finland youth international Glen made his eagerly anticipated first-team debut when he started the Capital One Cup clash at Sheffield Wednesday last season. The central midfielder had previously been named on the bench for the Champions League clash against Galatasaray in December 2014. But he got his chance at Hillsborough, playing an hour in the heart of the midfield and impressing with his discipline, robust tackling and tireless running. He turned 20 years old the following day. A product of the Arsenal academy, Glen has since gained more first-team experience during a loan spell with Southend United. He played six times in League One for the Shrimpers and will be hoping to build upon that exposure this season.

BORN:
FINLAND, OCTOBER 28, 1995

Arsenal at Euro

TEN ARSENAL PLAYERS WERE CALLED UP TO REPRESENT THEIR COUNTRIES AT EURO 2016 IN FRANCE. HERE'S HOW THEY GOT ON.

LAURENT KOSCIELNY
COUNTRY: FRANCE
ROUND REACHED: FINAL

Laurent played in all seven matches as France reached the final on home soil. He was one of their most consistent performers during the tournament, and spent longer on the pitch than any other Arsenal player – 642 minutes.

OLIVIER GIROUD
COUNTRY: FRANCE
ROUND REACHED: FINAL

After scoring the first goal of the tournament, during the opening day win over Romania, Olivier kept his place in the side and scored two more goals. They both came in the quarter-final win over Iceland, and he was duly named man-of-the-match. He claimed the Bronze Boot award, with a final tally of three goals and two assists.

2016

Aaron Ramsey
Country: Wales
Round reached: Semi-final

Aaron was named in UEFA's Official Team of the Tournament after helping Wales exceed expectations and reach the semi-final. No other player at Euro 2016 managed more than Aaron's four assists, and the midfielder also found the target in the 3-0 group stage win over Russia. He was, however, suspended for the semi-final, and Wales certainly missed him as they lost to eventual champions Portugal.

Mesut Ozil
Country: Germany
Round reached: Semi-final

Mesut was one of Germany's standout performers at the tournament, the highlights being his man-of-the-match performance against Northern Ireland and his fine goal against Italy in the quarter-final. He's the only player to score for Germany at each of the last four major international tournaments.

Wojciech Szczesny
Country: Poland
Round reached: Quarter-final

Wojciech started as Poland's number one goalkeeper, and he kept a clean sheet in the opening group stage win over Northern Ireland. Injury kept him out of the rest of the tournament though, and former Gunner Lukasz Fabianski took his place as Poland lost to eventual champions Portugal in the last eight.

JACK WILSHERE
COUNTRY: ENGLAND
ROUND REACHED: ROUND OF 16

The only Arsenal player in the England squad, Jack made three appearances at Euro 2016, coming on as a sub in the opening group stage win over Russia, then starting the goalless draw with Slovakia. He came on for the second half of the knockout round game against Iceland, but couldn't prevent Roy Hodgson's men from suffering a shock defeat.

GRANIT XHAKA
COUNTRY: SWITZERLAND
ROUND REACHED: ROUND OF 16

Arsenal's new signing was one of the stars of the group stage, winning UEFA's official man-of-the-match award in both Switzerland's win over Albania and the draw with Romania. The combative midfielder also started the Round of 16 game against Poland, but he missed the decisive penalty in the shoot out.

HECTOR BELLERIN
COUNTRY: SPAIN
ROUND REACHED: ROUND OF 16

Hector was called up to the Spain squad shortly after making his senior international debut in May. The right back was an unused sub though as the reigning champions crashed out to Italy in the Round of 16.

Euro 2016

Petr Cech
Country: Czech Republic
Round reached: Group stage

Petr played all three group games for the Czechs, but despite a great display in the opening match against Spain, he couldn't inspire his country to qualification. The goalkeeper announced his international retirement after the tournament, with a record 124 caps.

Tomas Rosicky
Country: Czech Republic
Round reached: Group stage

Still technically an Arsenal player during Euro 2016, Tomas's tournament was cut short by injury, before his country were eliminated at the group stage. The Czech captain did provide one moment of magic though, a superb cross for Milan Skoda to score in the 2-2 draw with Croatia.

Also...

Alexis Sanchez lifted silverware as Chile won the Copa America in dramatic fashion in June 2016. The Gunners forward was named Player of the Tournament, scoring three goals as Chile retained the trophy after beating Argentina in the final. Staged in the United States, David Ospina and Joel Campbell also impressed at the competition, for Colombia and Costa Rica respectively.

Premier League All-Stars

CAN YOU FIND THE PLAYERS WHO HAVE PLAYED MORE THAN 200 TIMES FOR ARSENAL IN THE PREMIER LEAGUE?

```
W A L H H I K E O W N K B E R
R B L A F O N X I D P M A K G
E G A J S N R U B R E T N I W
N W W I U E I V N W O K N E H
A I I N T N E N O X I D R E E
M B T L J U G P A R L E Y R A
A U N O B F A B R E G A S A S
E R E H U E N A E T U O A E R
S S G A S R R M Y R E R G M U
S M R E A A E R V A G V N A O
G A B F F A N N G E S K A T L
R D X O D E A G A K S I A W R
E A I D H U R S P M A N T M A
B K A M P O A R I E I V E A P
W A L C O T T B M A D A O C L
```

ADAMS	*PARLOUR*
BERGKAMP	*SAGNA*
DIXON	*SEAMAN*
FABREGAS	*TOURE*
HENRY	*VIEIRA*
KEOWN	*WALCOTT*
LJUNGBERG	*WINTERBURN*

Answers on p.61

Arsenal Competition

ANSWER THE FOLLOWING QUESTION CORRECTLY AND YOU COULD WIN AN ARSENAL FC SHIRT SIGNED BY A FIRST TEAM PLAYER.

JOE FROM HERTFORDSHIRE, LAST YEAR'S COMPETITION WINNER.

NEW FOR 2016/2017

Who scored Arsenal's first goal of the 2016/17 season?

A. Alex Oxlade-Chamberlain
B. Alexis Sanchez
C. Theo Walcott

Entry is by email only. Only one entry per contestant. Please enter AFC SHIRT followed by either A, B or C in the subject line of an email. In the body of the email, please include your full name, address, postcode, email address and phone number and send to: **frontdesk@grangecommunications.co.uk** by Friday 31 March 2017.

Terms and Conditions

These terms and conditions ("Terms and Conditions") set out the basis on which you can participate in the Arsenal 2016/17 Season Shirt Competition ("Competition"). By entering the Competition, you accept these Terms and Conditions in full. If you do not accept these Terms and Conditions, you should not enter the Competition and you will not be eligible to win the prize. Entry is by email only.

1. COMPETITION PERIOD: The start date for entries is Monday 3rd October 2016 at 16:00 (UK time) ("Start Date"). The closing date for entries is Friday 31st March 2017 at midnight (UK time) ("Closing Date"). Entries received after the Closing Date will not be entered into the Competition. 2. TO ENTER: To enter the Competition, you need to answer the following question: Who scored Arsenal's first goal of the 2016/17 season? A. Alex Oxlade-Chamberlain B. Alexis Sanchez C. Theo Walcott. Please enter AFC SHIRT followed by either A, B or C in the subject line of an email. In the body of the email, please include your full name, address, postcode, email address and phone number and send to: frontdesk@ grangecommunications.co.uk by Friday 31 March 2017. 3. ELIGIBILITY: Entry is open to UK residents only. Only one entry per person is allowed. 4. If entrants are under 18, consent from a parent or guardian must be obtained prior to entry and the parent or guardian must agree to these Terms and Conditions in full. 5. Employees of The Arsenal Football Club Plc (company number 109244) ("Arsenal"), the Promoter or members of their immediate families are not eligible to enter the Competition. 6. Entry is by email only. No purchase is required to enter but you will require email and internet access to enter the Competition. No refund may be claimed for any expenses incurred relating to the use of an email account or internet connection for the purpose of entering the Competition. 7. PRIZE: There will be one prize of an Arsenal 2016/17 season football shirt signed by at least one player for Arsenal's first team (the "Prize"). The Prize is non-transferable and no cash alternative will be offered. 8. SELECTION OF WINNER: The winner will be picked at random from all eligible and correct entries received between the Start Date and the Closing Date. 9. The winner will be contacted using the contact details provided on entry within 72 hours of the Closing Date. If the winner cannot be contacted or does not respond to confirm details for delivery of the Prize within 21 days, an alternative winner will be selected at random from the remaining eligible and correct entries. 10. Unless otherwise notified to the winner, the Prize will be delivered to the winner within 30 days of confirmation of the winner's address for delivery of the Prize. 11. PUBLICITY AND PERSONAL DATA: If the winner is aged 18 or over, the winner agrees to take part in reasonable publicity relating to the Competition and the Promoter and Arsenal may use the winner's name and image and his/her comments relating to the Competition and/or the Prize for future promotional, marketing and publicity purposes in any media worldwide without notice and without any fee being paid. 12. Details of the winner's name and county will be available on request for one month after the Closing Date by writing to the Promoter (including providing a stamped self-addressed envelope) at the address set out below. 13. The Promoter will use entrants' personal details for the purposes of administering the Competition and awarding the Prize. The Promoter may also pass on entrants' details to Arsenal, who may use the details to contact entrants about Arsenal's products and services, in accordance with Arsenal's privacy policy, available at http://www.arsenal.com/privacy-policy. By entering the Competition, you are indicating your agreement to this unless you tell us otherwise. If you do not wish to be contacted or to receive marketing information, you can opt out at any time by emailing AFC STOP to frontdesk@grangecommunications.co.uk. 14. OTHER IMPORTANT INFORMATION: Entries must not be submitted through agents or third parties. No responsibility can be accepted for lost, delayed, incomplete, or for electronic entries or winning notifications that are not received or delivered (for any reason including as a consequence of communication or network failures). Any such entries will be deemed void. 15. The Promoter reserves the right to withdraw or amend the Competition or these Terms and Conditions if circumstances outside its reasonable control make this unavoidable. 16. Entries must be strictly in accordance with these Terms and Conditions. Any entry not in strict accordance with these Terms and Conditions will be deemed to be invalid and the Prize will not be awarded in respect of such entry. The Promoter reserves the right to verify the eligibility of any entrant and to exclude any entries which it believes to be invalid or in breach of these Terms and Conditions. 17. The Promoter's decision is final in all matters relating to the Competition (including the Prize) and no correspondence will be entered into. 18. Except in respect of death or personal injury resulting from any negligence of Arsenal, to the maximum extent permitted by law, neither Arsenal nor any of its officers, employees or agents shall be responsible for (whether in tort, contract or otherwise): i) any loss, damage or injury to you and/or any third party or to any property belonging to you or any third party in connection with the Competition and/or the Prize (including the winner's receipt or use of the same), resulting from any cause whatsoever; or ii) any loss of profit, loss of use, loss of opportunity or any indirect, economic or consequential losses whatsoever and howsoever caused. 19. GOVERNING LAW AND JURISDICTION: The Competition, and any dispute or claim arising out of or in connection with it, shall be governed by and construed in accordance with English law. You irrevocably agree that the courts of England and Wales shall have exclusive jurisdiction to settle any dispute or claim that arises out of or in connection with the Competition. 20. SPIRIT OF THE COMPETITION: If you attempt to compromise the integrity or proper operation of the Competition by cheating or committing fraud in any way, the Promoter and Arsenal each reserve the right to render your entry invalid, seek damages from you and ban you from participating in any of their future competitions. 21. CONTACT: If you have any questions about the Competition, please contact the Promoter. 22. PROMOTER: The Promoter of the Competition is Grange Communications Ltd, 22 Great King Street, Edinburgh EH3 6QH ("Promoter") on behalf of Arsenal.

True or False?

LOOK AT THESE FOUR PICTURES AND WORK OUT WHICH OF THE STATEMENTS ABOUT THEM ARE TRUE AND WHICH ARE FALSE.

A

1. This picture of Dennis Bergkamp was taken at the end of the invincibles season 2003/04. _____

2. Bergkamp never scored a hat-trick for Arsenal. _____

3. Bergkamp has more Premier League assists for Arsenal than any other player. _____

B

1. This statue is based on Thierry Henry's celebration after scoring against Tottenham Hotspur. _____

2. Arsenal never lost when Henry scored in a game at Highbury. _____

3. The last six goals of Henry's Arsenal career were all headers. _____

C

1. This photo is of Aaron Ramsey celebrating his goal against Aston Villa in the 2014 FA Cup final. _____

2. Half of all Arsenal's FA Cup final wins have come under Arsène Wenger. _____

3. Ramsey is the only Welshman to play for Arsenal in the Premier League. _____

D

1. This photo was taken at White Hart Lane last season. _____

2. Arsenal have never finished below Tottenham under Arsène Wenger. _____

3. Hector Bellerin left Barcelona in the same month that Alexis Sanchez signed for the Spanish side. _____

Answers on p.61

Mesut Ozil's
Dream XI

We asked our players to be manager for a day, and choose their ultimate XI.

GOALKEEPER
IKER CASILLAS
He belongs among the best goalkeepers in the world.

RIGHT BACK
PHILIPP LAHM
A sensational player who has won many trophies.

CENTRE BACK
SERGIO RAMOS
For me he's the best centre back in the world.

CENTRE BACK
JEROME BOATENG
He also belongs among the best defenders in the world in my opinion.

LEFT BACK
MARCELO
I've never seen another defender as technically gifted as Marcelo.

CENTRE MIDFIELD
XABI ALONSO
I've never seen another player with his ability to play such fantastic passes.

NUMBER 10
SERGE GNABRY
I'm including him in my team because he is sitting right next to me at the moment!

CENTRE MIDFIELD
SANTI CAZORLA
He's just outstanding technically.

RIGHT WING
ANGEL DI MARIA
He's another who is outstanding technically.

CENTRE FORWARD
KARIM BENZEMA
For me he's the most complete striker.

LEFT WING
CRISTIANO RONALDO
He scores lots of goals and he's very ambitious too.

Numbers Game

MATCH THE PLAYERS TO HOW MANY GAMES THEY HAD PLAYED FOR ARSENAL BY THE START OF THE CURRENT SEASON.

HECTOR BELLERIN

16

PETR CECH

187

344

MOHAMED ELNENY

OLIVIER GIROUD

248

LAURENT KOSCIELNY

MESUT OZIL

73

117

149

THEO WALCOTT

ALEX OXLADE-CHAMBERLAIN

42

Answers on p.61

Diary Dates

IN WHICH MONTH DID THE FOLLOWING EVENTS ALL TAKE PLACE?

1 ROBERT PIRES was born (1973). ARSÈNE WENGER became Arsenal manager (1996), THIERRY HENRY became Arsenal's record scorer (2005).

2 RAY PARLOUR made his debut (1992), THEO WALCOTT signed for Arsenal (2006), JACK WILSHERE was born (1992).

3 DENNIS BERGKAMP was born (1969), ARSENAL won the Premier League title (2002), ARSENAL played their last ever game at Highbury (2006).

4 THIERRY HENRY signed for Arsenal (1999), ARSENAL won the Community Shield (2004), JACK WILSHERE made his England debut (2010).

5 NICOLAS ANELKA signed (1997), ARSENAL beat Barcelona at Emirates Stadium (2011), THIERRY HENRY scored his final Arsenal goal (2012).

6 ARSENAL played their first ever league game (1893), PER MERTESACKER was born (1984), MESUT OZIL made his Arsenal debut (2013).

7 ARSENAL recorded their record league win (1900), HECTOR BELLERIN was born (1995), DENNIS BERGKAMP scored a wonder goal against Newcastle (2002).

8 ARSENAL was formed (1886), SANTI CAZORLA was born (1984), JOHN JENSEN scored his only Arsenal goal (1994).

9 TONY ADAMS made his debut (1983), DANNY WELBECK was born (1990), ARSENAL beat Inter Milan at the San Siro (2003).

10 ARSENAL won the league title at Stamford Bridge (1933), FREDDIE LJUNGBERG was born (1977), ARSENAL beat Tottenham in the FA Cup semi-final at Wembley (1993).

Answers on p.61

JUNIOR GUNNERS is the youth membership for young Arsenal fans, and the only way you can get access to tickets, fun events with players and weekly competitions. Junior Gunners is for fans aged from 0 to 16 years old, and depending on your age you get different events and competitions offered to you. **Membership starts from £10 per season; the perfect way to join the Arsenal family!**

DISCOUNTED TICKETS!

ACCESS TO ARSENAL PLAYERS

CHANCES TO MEET YOUR HEROS!

REGULAR E-NEWSLETTERS AND NEWSLETTERS IN THE POST

EXCLUSIVE EVENTS AND AWESOME COMPETITIONS

BE PART OF THE BALL SQUAD

BIRTHDAY AND CHRISTMAS CARDS

THE CHANCE TO BE A MASCOT

YOUR OWN JUNIOR GUNNERS APP

10% OFF ARSENAL SOCCER SCHOOLS

JOIN NOW AT:
ALWAYSAHEADOFTHEGAME.COM/JUNIOR

Quiz and Puzzle Answers

P.23 SPOT THE BALL

P.31 49ERS QUIZ

1. True (Jermaine Pennant and Robert Pires)
2. Thierry Henry
3. Pascal Cygan
4. 2-2
5. Patrick Vieira
6. Middlesbrough
7. 36 (13 draws)

P.33 EMIRATES STADIUM TRIVIA

1. Gilberto
2. South
3. Tony Adams
4. Tottenham Hotspur
5. Theo Walcott
6. 60,272
7. Brazil
8. Arsenal
9. True
10. 2006
11. Two
12. 3-0

P.54 WORDSEARCH

P.56 TRUE OR FALSE?

Picture A:
1. True
2. False
   (he scored one)
3. True (94)

Picture B:
1. True
2. False
3. False

Picture C:
1. False
   (it was against Hull City)
2. True (six out of 12)
3. False

Picture D:
1. True
2. True
3. True (July 2011)

P.58 NUMBERS GAME

Theo Walcott 344
Laurent Koscielny 248
Olivier Giroud 187
Alex Oxlade-Chamberlain 149

Mesut Ozil 117
Hector Bellerin 73
Petr Cech 42
Mohamed Elneny 16

P.59 DIARY DATES

1. October
2. January
3. May
4. August
5. February

6. September
7. March
8. December
9. November
10. April

Where's Gunnersaurus?